LOST

LOST YOUTH

A World War II Memoir

Michael J. DeSalis

Copyright © 2013 by Michael J. DeSalis.

Library of Congress Control Number: 2013901996
ISBN: Hardcover   978-1-4797-8870-5
              Softcover   978-1-4797-8869-9
              Ebook   978-1-4797-8871-2

All rights reserved. No part of this book may be reproduced or transmitted in any form or by any means, electronic or mechanical, including photocopying, recording, or by any information storage and retrieval system, without permission in writing from the copyright owner.

Copyedited by Katrina Fernando
Reviewed by Fatimah Imam

This book was printed in the United States of America.

To order additional copies of this book, contact:
Xlibris Corporation
1-888-795-4274
www.Xlibris.com
Orders@Xlibris.com

This story is lovingly dedicated to Denise, Michele, Michael, and Lisa, my loyal and faithful children who watched me from the windows of heaven while I suffered the loss of my youth.

TABLE OF CONTENTS

I	Volunteer	1
II	Humiliation	3
III	Evaluation	6
IV	Exercise	8
V	Volunteer Again	10
VI	Purchase Orders	11
VII	South Dakota State College	12
VIII	Myrtle Beach, South Carolina	16
IX	Tennessee	17
X	Sharpshooter	20
XI	Army WACs	22
XII	Now to California	23
XIII	Marriage/Adultery	25
XIV	All Aboard	26
XV	Conte di Savoia	27
XVI	Storm	30
XVII	Starvation	31
XVIII	Burlesque	32
XIX	Australia Entertainment	33
XX	New Zealand Apples	34
XXI	Bombay	35
XXII	Reincarnation	36
XXIII	Missionaries	37
XXIV	Unload	38
XXV	Jorhat, India	39
XXVI	Driver's License	40
XXVII	Chinese Friends	41

XXVIII	Ennui	44
XXIX	Another Tragedy	45
XXX	Monsoon	46
XXXI	Banded Krait Snake	47
XXXII	Cowboys and Indians	49
XXXIII	Childhood Tragedy	50
XXXIV	Dumbo and Company	51
XXXV	Meeting a Friend/Foe	53
XXXVI	Thirty Days' Punishment	55
XXXVII	Burma Next to Last	56
XXXVIII	Salty Kool-Aid	58
XXXIX	Calcutta	59
XL	Kitty	60
XLI	No Chutes	62
XLII	Kitty Again	63
XLIII	Darjeeling	65
XLIV	Bathtub	67
XLV	Horseback Rides	68
XLVI	Donkeys	69
XLVII	Hobby	70
XLVIII	Burma Hijacking	71
XLIX	VE Day	72
L	Poor Nurses	73
LI	Karachi Seaport	76
LII	Going Home	77
LIII	Stringer	79
LIV	Movie Time—Nice Marines	80
LV	Happy New Year	81
LVI	Home!	83
LVII	Foolhardy	85

Epilogue 87

CHAPTER I

Volunteer

IT IS NOVEMBER 1942. I find myself in a nondescript former government office probably used in World War I by the Selective Service System. Why am I here? It is rumored that the National Draft Board has discontinued all enlistments. Those who would like to volunteer would then be given a V number and permitted to officially volunteer for service. The volunteers would then be able to choose their branch of service after being notified that they would be sworn in on a specific date and then sent to basic training. That's what I did. I was notified that I would be sworn in on January 16, 1943, and sent to basic training on January 23, 1943. I was happy with that because I knew that I could choose my branch of service. I had already decided that I wanted the Air Corps, so "off we go into the wild blue yonder." Shortly afterward, I received a notice to report to an armory on January 16, 1943, for swearing in. This was followed by departure by rail on January 23, 1943, to New Cumberland, Pennsylvania, for basic training. Up until this time, I had no fear of what the future might hold.

On January 16, my father and I went to the armory, and there I was along with hundreds of other poor souls. We were given a lunch ticket and told to report to the armory at 1:00 p.m. where we would be sworn in. During the swearing in, I noticed that my father was standing on the outside of the building with his nose pressed against the window of the door. Looking back on that moment, I am sure that it had to be one of the hardest things for him to see. His young eighteen-year-old son enlisted to go to war, and there was nothing he could do to ensure that he would return safely.

CHAPTER II

Humiliation

ON JANUARY 23, as ordered, I went to the railroad station accompanied by my parents, who by this time were not too happy about the fact that I had volunteered for the service. After tearful good-byes, I got on the train, and after about an hour and a half, we stopped at Harrisburg, Pennsylvania, the capital of the state where we detrained. We were then marched into an armory and told to drop our pants. We were given no information as to what was going on, and what they were about to do was very humiliating. Then a medical officer proceeded to begin the process of examining our privates, looking for disease or whatnot. It was at that very moment that I knew I had made a fatal mistake in volunteering for the service. This was a foreshadowing of what was to come.

From there we continued on to New Cumberland, Pennsylvania, for the beginning of our basic training. We were put into barracks, each having cots and a wood stove. Remember, this was in the middle of January, and one wood stove was not enough to make us all warm. The people in uniform who were in charge made us do ridiculous things like get up at 6:30 a.m. and go out in our underwear to do calisthenics. We would then put on our clothes and go into the mess hall, which was really a mess, for cold food and cold coffee. In the midst of all this was a lot of cursing and shouting, criticizing our inability to do calisthenics properly or by their standards; these were not nice people. At night, instead of going to sleep, card tables were brought out for cards and dice—the uniforms were apparently prepared to have us enjoy ourselves with some gambling. Remember, we were mostly eighteen-year-olds with not a lot of money, but enough to make the uniforms happy. The night started with card games and dice, and before the night was over, the uniforms had taken all the money away from us. This was the second fatal mistake that I made for volunteering. The next morning, we were up in the dark in our underwear, running around like madmen, and then into the mess hall for cold breakfast and cold coffee, followed by more calisthenics. This was unbelievable to me; there was no hope for the future. The gambling went on until there was no more money. There was a movie theater on the base, and I remember going to a movie one night since I had nothing else to do. I saw a movie with somebody named Perry Como, who was new to me. The movie was not very good, but it did pass the time.

We did this for several days with still no uniforms. I guess it was naive to think having uniforms would make a difference, but by the third or fourth day, they issued uniforms. We stood in line, and somebody would throw a pair of pants, shirts, socks, shoes, and jackets to you without regard to size, but they were pretty close to what you needed to make up the military uniform and hoping they would fit.

We were given light-yellow piping and told to have it sewn on our overseas caps, which would indicate we were in the Medical Corps. I got very upset when I heard this because I thought I had my choice of the Army Air Corps, which is why I had volunteered, and when I complained about it, I was laughed at by the uniforms. We weren't allowed to volunteer for the Air Corps, the Marine Corps, or anything, so that was not true. Volunteering did not give us anything. We then went to the local tailor who they told us we should use, who over charged us, but he had a captive audience.

By this time, it was Friday and we were told we could call our parents, and they could come to New Cumberland to see their sons. They were only away from us for a short time, but most of the parents came. My parents came, and we spent the day walking around the base aimlessly. The uniform made a difference to them and to me. Then I had to see them off, and there were more tearful good-byes. Later, my uncle told me that my father was very upset after leaving, and despite the fact that he was never very emotional, they could not calm him down. I think he was so upset to see his son in a situation that he could not change, and it could possibly have been the last time he saw me. We didn't know what the future held, but there were a lot of thoughts in our heads, as well as the heads of our parents. So in order to be able to continue, I sort of went into a trance from that point on, as it was the only way that I could cope.

CHAPTER III

Evaluation

WE WENT THROUGH a process where they physically, mentally, and psychologically evaluated us. I was taken into a typewriter room with about twenty typewriters arranged next to each other on a single table. I was given a piece of paper, and I was told when to start typing. Without thinking, I started to type, but the typewriters were so close together that when I returned the carriage, they bumped into each other and the one on the end of the table fell on the floor. It wasn't funny at the time for I was trying to type, but I was unable to gather any speed under the circumstances. The evaluator rated me as semiskilled. When I graduated high school, I could type one hundred words a minute, which was very good, but now I am being told I am semiskilled. I showed the evaluator a letter of recommendation that I received from the colonel at the Ordinance Department of the Frankford Arsenal in Philadelphia, who recommended me very strongly because of the work I did. The evaluator read the letter and scoffed at me and said, "You couldn't possibly have done all this." That was the extent of it.

After several days of this insanity, we were loaded on a train with the destination unknown. It turned out that we were going south to St. Petersburg, Florida, where the real basic training began. The train ride was uneventful except for the fact that an army wife—there were also civilians on the train—was going to visit her husband, who had recently joined the service. She climbed in an upper berth with some GIs. When I heard about this, it disgusted me. But as I matured, I realized that was life. We were put up in a very nice hotel, which was going to be our home for the next eight weeks. We started out with calisthenics and marching around and around. We had to sing songs, some which I had never heard of and some I had, like "Wild Blue Yonder." They wanted us to sing as loud as we could. One day, I saw a very large sign telling the people in the town that they should be glad that we were there marching by their homes because we were training to save them and save democracy. The commanding general of the base apparently had some complaints about the singing waking up the old folks who were retired in Florida.

CHAPTER IV

Exercise

WE HAD TO run around like fools and sing and shout and march and march. The punishment for fouling up (which they had another word for) was stiff. You had to run around in the sand like an idiot with a rifle above your head. You dig ditches and then fill them up again. Being in the army was like being in a trance, and sometimes it was hard to get out of that because of all the shouting and cursing. We did the fifty-yard dash, push-ups, sit-ups, and every foolishness devised by man to find out what you are like when you began and then to do it all over again to see how you improved. Older people really couldn't take it, and often you see some thirty-year-old young man passed out from the exertion. The uniforms really got a kick out of that and would ridicule anybody who couldn't take it.

If you are expecting to hear some really sordid war stories, I think you are out of luck because this is more psychological fantasies or what could happen when a person makes a fatal mistake.

After two months of this basic training, we were put into trucks and ended up in Clearwater, Florida, which was the spring training home of the National League Phillies baseball team and my hometown team. The army had taken over their hotel, and that is where we lived for the next four months of training—on a golf course in a beautiful hotel. Of course, the army botched up the golf course, and the greens and the fairways were just mud. We continued to do more marching and marching and running and running. There were many lectures, and once, I fell asleep during one and was punished by being made to stand at attention for two hours, and as you were falling asleep, someone would grab you. It was torture.

CHAPTER V

Volunteer Again

ONE DAY, A noncommissioned officer asked for a volunteer bugler, of all things, because at six o'clock they lowered the flag and had some kind of ceremony. When I was a teenager, I learned to play the bugle and trumpet, so I volunteered, even though no one ever volunteered for anything in the service. Nobody knew the army bugle calls, so I found myself at six o'clock the next day ready to do whatever they asked. At the end of the ceremony, a lieutenant said to me, "Six o'clock tomorrow, be here." I knew that respect is supposed to be given to the officers or even the noncommissioned officers; however, the next day I told the lieutenant that I didn't join the army to become a bugler and I was not going to be there at six o'clock tomorrow. I added that I enjoyed the Army Drum and Bugle Corps, which I saw marching up and down the perimeter of the basic training camp. I told him that if I were given an audition, I was sure that they would want me to join because I was pretty good. The lieutenant turned around and walked away. That was the end of my career as a bugler. In retrospect, that was very foolish of me because I probably could have been transferred into the bugle corps and could have had a pretty posh job.

CHAPTER VI

Purchase Orders

ONE DAY, ONE of the uniforms picked me for some reason and asked me if I would help him with this purchase order. It turned out there was a great deal of administrative paperwork associated with supplies. So I followed him around for a few days, then he said he was going to try and get me transferred to him so that I could help him with all the work that needed to be done. Unfortunately, that never came to fruition.

CHAPTER VII

South Dakota State College

BASIC TRAINING FINALLY ended, and we were taken to the train station, not being told where we were going of course, and we went north.

Whenever you went north in those days, you had to go through Chicago and change trains. Then we took another train, which took us to South Dakota, of all places. I had heard of the Black Hills of South Dakota, where the soil was black and could grow anything. We pulled into a train station in Brookings, South Dakota, which turned out to be the South Dakota State College. The army had taken over the college; however, they continued to teach women, so there were four hundred women and four hundred GIs. Can you imagine that? There was a dance for the new students, where I met a good-looking girl and made some time with her. It turned out that she was a secretary to the colonel of the whole school. You were not allowed to meet the girls after the dance, but we made arrangements to find each other somewhere. So for the entire time I was at the college, she was my girlfriend. In her apartment, she had a liquor cabinet, and I had a key to her apartment. So whenever I had time off, which wasn't much, I had a place to live.

A funny incident happened when we were on the train, ready to go to another base where we would be stationed after the school training. My girlfriend came running down the railroad tracks and fell, ripping her stockings and scraping her knees, with blood running down her legs, and she was crying. It was like something out of a John Garfield movie.

When we got there, the lieutenant who greeted us said, "You'll never, in your army career, be as lucky as you are today. You'll find when you leave here you'll be digging ditches in Tennessee, but here you are going to college and you're going to enjoy it." We were assigned two to a room of a newly built, beautiful dormitory. We didn't know why we were there, but it turned out we were there to take administrative courses in army administration.

During that time, I devised a system so that the office personnel could easily determine the location of each enlisted man. The captain in charge recognized the importance of my system when we first arrived, and he appointed me to be in charge of the four hundred students for the entire two weeks we were in South Dakota. This was quite surreal because when my parents viewed the graduation exercises, they saw their little boy leading the entire four hundred men marching like a big deal. Then again, they were used to seeing me leading the band as a drum major when I was in high school, but here I was in an army uniform, which was so impressive to them.

One of the courses was typing, and in high school I could type one hundred words a minute, which was excellent speed, so I was already a typist. At one point, we were asked to apply for Officer Candidate School, to which I did, and I was picked especially due to the fact that the captain remembered that I devised the student system. All the candidates marched down the streets of Brookings, South Dakota, and you never saw such marching in your life. Nobody said a word because everyone was so overwhelmed that they were going to make Officer Candidate School. We went into a building where there was a panel of about six major officers: lieutenant, lieutenant colonel, and colonel. We were ushered in one at a time, and the panel asked questions. There I was, an eighteen-year-old, and they were asking me ridiculous questions. At the end of the interview, I thought the officer in charge asked me if I had any questions, and I answered, "No, sir"; however, he was asking the panel. I think that ruined my chances for Officer Candidate School, but at least I had the opportunity. Not too many men were chosen.

Later, in one of my insane moments a couple of years later, I found myself filling out an application for paratrooper school. I am sure I was demented at the time, but luckily I was not chosen.

South Dakota State College is located in Brookings, South Dakota. During World War II, it was used by the US Army as an administration school, housing four hundred troops for each semester.

CHAPTER VIII

Myrtle Beach, South Carolina

WE FINALLY FINISHED our courses in South Dakota State College. And as the train pulled out of the station, we had to wait until we were on our way to nowhere before we were allowed to open up our orders on the train. The oldest person in the group was given the orders and told us we were going to Myrtle Beach, South Carolina. It was a long train ride that took a couple of days, and you had to change trains to get into Myrtle Beach, which was a one-horse town. Back then it had a Toonerville trolley to get into the town. The trolley took about forty-five minutes with a coal stove in the middle, which we huddled around to get warm. Once we got there, we found out they had no accommodations for us, so we had to find rooms in rooming houses. They gave us a couple of vouchers for meals, but there was only one restaurant, called the Cozy Corner, which was a greasy spoon. Today there are over two hundred restaurants and more golf courses than you can imagine.

We then found out we were going to be trained to rescue downed pilots in either the Atlantic or Pacific Ocean. It didn't take me long to decide how to get out of this. I was not a good swimmer, and I was about to be drowned if I was going to have this training. So I was assigned instead to a squadron that was ready for overseas duty. I met myself coming around the corner, which I often did.

CHAPTER IX

Tennessee

SO AFTER A couple of weeks of meals at the Cozy Corner and living in a rooming house, we were on our way by train to Dyersburg, Tennessee. There was a private first class in charge of us, and we were still like being civilians and we have nobody to answer to until we arrived at Dyersburg. We reported to the captain of our squadron, who was from Pittsburg. He acted like we were neighbors because we both came from three hundred miles away. We found ourselves in a real army. The worst thing about it was when the squadron people realized we were promoted to PFC and they were still privates, even after being in the army for a longer period of time, they were not happy. Needless to say, they did everything they could to make us uncomfortable. For example, the first night, they put us on guard duty, and we had to walk through the area with rifles, helmets, and backpacks as we waited for someone to jump out of the darkness and attack us. We were scared out of our wits, and after a six-hour period of guard duty, we flopped in our cots. The next morning, we began our new duty, and we got separated into three or four locations. One was Chattanooga, Tennessee, where I spent some time that I enjoyed because it was much more of a cosmopolitan city. There I met a girl at a USO dance, but she had a boyfriend who was in the Army Dance Band, and he was not too pleased when he saw us talking. Then, one of the other members of the squadron said he knew a girl with a friend. I then found myself at the apartment with my buddy and these two girls. I thought we were golden, but during the night, the phone rang in the bedroom of my girl. It turned out that it was her boyfriend who was in the service somewhere. After the phone call was over, I tried my best, but nothing happened. She said, "The next time you come back it will be better, but I'm not feeling too well tonight." So I got the gist of that statement and was happy that she said I could come back. However, that never happened, and I never did go back. That was the extent of my fun in Chattanooga.

TENNESSEE STATE FLAG

The three stars on the flag represent the three different land forms in Tennessee: mountains in the east, highlands in the middle, and lowlands in the west. On the flag, these regions are bound together in an unbroken circle. The field is crimson with a blue background for the stars. The final blue strip relieves the sameness of the crimson field and prevents the flag from showing too much crimson when it is limp.

CHAPTER X

Sharpshooter

THE NEXT TIME we left, it was for a three-day-and-night adventure in the wilderness, where we slept in two-man tents and dug ditches then filled them back up. We were out on the firing range, which was about three hundred yards to the targets. We were using M1 rifles, which are very heavy, and when you pull the trigger, it would ricochet back into your shoulder, and it hurt very much. I fired one hundred rounds, and out of the seventy-six of us who fired, they said that I came in second. I don't know how that happened. The highest score was one hundred, and I don't know what my score was, but they said we were going to compete the next day. The one who would win first prize would get $100 and a promotion. I made a mistake telling somebody in charge I wanted to go back to the base camp to get my glasses. Since I had come in second with no glasses, they didn't accommodate me.

Then we had to hike twenty miles and then hike back to camp. As we trotted back to camp, some of us went into the shower room because we were so dirty, which was not allowed. I was punished for that, which was the beginning of many punishments I received due to my trying to push the limits of the rules.

One night, we were allowed off the base to go to the movies or eat or whatever we wanted to do. So I got on the army bus, which took us into town, and when we got there, I had to go to the bathroom really bad. So I went into the movie theater and paid my way to get in, but just so I could go to the bathroom. I didn't see the movie. I was always trying to get away from the army discipline. Then, after going around town all night, we headed back to catch the army bus, but it had already left to return to camp. We had no way to get back, but then someone offered us the opportunity to stand on the rear bumper of an old-fashioned car, which we had to grip on with our fingers—and the guy was driving recklessly—but finally arrived back at camp after a forty-five-minute ride. We could have been killed.

CHAPTER XI

Army WACs

WE WERE THEN relocated near Fort Oglethorpe, Georgia, which was the training camp of the WACs,(Women's Army Corps) and we would occasionally see the women. We were taken to a USO dance, and sure enough, most of the women were overweight. The lieutenant in charge was a thirty to thirty-five-year-old woman who was also overweight. Watching them do calisthenics was hilarious. So all seventy-six of us were taken to the dance floor where we danced the night away. There was also some drinking even though many of us were underage. I didn't drink. The lieutenant lady sure got tipsy, and she was falling all over the GIs who were privates, PFCs and sergeants. At the end of the night, we all piled into a two-half ton truck to be driven back to Fort Oglethorpe, about thirty miles away. We got the girls to sit on our laps—of each one we could manage—and tried to fondle them while they asked us where we were from. One of the girls was from Delaware, so we were talking and she grabbed on to me and I was trying to fondle her. We finally got back to Fort Oglethorpe, and we piled out of the truck. The girl and I went into the WACs barracks, and some were on the top bunk while others were on the bottom. Mostly everyone had been drinking, and they were very drunk. One of the WACs fell off her upper bunk and broke her neck. We then somehow got out of there and got back to our camp. It wasn't a good night.

CHAPTER XII

Now to California

IT WAS TIME again to leave and go to our next location, which happened to be Riverside, California, where we prepared to get on a ship to go overseas. The train ride was several days, and we were fed out of vats of soup on the train, sitting in our seats. The soup was steaming hot, and it was very difficult to try and eat while the train moved back and forth, but it was the only food we got, so we had to figure out how to eat it.

We then arrived in Riverside, and another train pulled alongside of us, and all the windows on the train were blacked out. We all wondered what that was all about. Pretty soon we found out that the windows were black because there were German prisoners of war on the train. They were taken from Italy, France, or Germany to the United States, where they were fed real food, and we were going in the opposite direction, to the war. I think it would have been better to be a prisoner of war than to be an American GI going into war at that time. We were then assigned to barracks where we had to go through some stupid training. For example, one of the things that we had to learn was to climb over the side of a ship in case we had to abandon ship. It was a wooden platform that was about forty feet high, and the day before we were going to this training, I went up to the top level, looked down, and got cold chills. The next day we had to dress with a full field backpack, rifle, helmet, and gas mask with whatever junk they had for us to wear. We had to climb over the barrier at the top and go down the side of this makeshift side of the ship that was fixed with vertical and horizontal ropes. You had to hold on to the vertical ropes when you went down very gingerly. During the descent, one of the wise guys in the squadron, whom I didn't like, froze in fear and was unable to move. They had to lower him down with some kind of a crane with a net. After that, surprisingly, nobody made fun of him or said anything nasty, realizing that we were also scared. I was surprised that I managed to make the descent, but I guess when you're scared out of your wits, you'll do anything.

CHAPTER XIII

Marriage/Adultery

THE CAPTAIN IN charge of us was getting married while we were in Riverside. She was from Pennsylvania, and she came out there to get married before he went overseas. The day of the marriage, I was honored to have the responsibility of washing his car, which I really didn't like doing, so I didn't do a good job of wiping it out. They had a military wedding in a church, and we had swords to hold up in an arch as they walked under the swords. Five days after the wedding, we were ready to leave camp and get on the ship, and his wife had already gone home. There to see him off was one of the army nurses whom he had met in Riverside and was messing around with before he got married. The nurse was kissing him like she was out of her mind, and they were all over each other. Seeing this at my immature young age, I thought that it was a terrible thing to do, but in this case, I might have done the same thing.

CHAPTER XIV

All Aboard

THEY TOOK ROLL call, and we were put on a gangplank to walk up to the ship with large duffel bags that were very heavy. Most of us got on okay except for one poor soul who dropped his duffel bag into the water under the gangplank. Now we were on our way once again, and we didn't have the slightest idea about our destination.

CHAPTER XV

Conte di Savoia

THIS SHIP WAS enormous, with two smoke stacks. It happened to be an Italian luxury liner that was taken over by the United States when it was in New York, when war was declared. The Americans took over and made it into a troop ship, holding about 4,500 men, to be used to send people like me overseas. It was called the *Conte di Savoia*. The most beautiful room in the ship was the big dining room, which was paneled with mahogany, and they put books in it. It was reserved for the army MPs to sleep due to their stressful duties. I was put six floors down, at the bottom of the ship, and each man there had a bunk bed that would roll with the bumps of the sea. They were held with chains, so you couldn't push your bed against the wall. There was no air down there, and it was so stifling we would sleep under the sleeve of canvas about ten feet in circumference so the air would come down from the top of the ship. We spent most of every day lying on the floor underneath to get some air. Every once in a while, there would be an alarm, and the wheel door would be locked. We were told that there was a submarine following us. If we got hit in one part of the ship, it could be divided into three parts, so the rest of the ship would still be able to continue to stay afloat. The marines that were in charge would walk around with sidearms, cursing and screaming at everybody. One night, I was lying on top of the deck on the steel floor to get some sleep, and I heard a marine come by. I knew without opening my eyes, and he kicked me and said, "He looks like he's dead."

From the very first day on the ship, I decided that my squadron will be looking for me every day to give me the worst jobs, like KP (Kitchen Police), so I decided never to sleep in my bunk. So I spent most nights on deck since the weather was very good, even though sometimes it got very hot, so I could get away with it. One day, I saw an army MP with whom I had gone to high school, and I talked to him and we were very good friends. I was telling him some of my troubles, and he said, "When I work the night shift, you can sleep in my bunk in the dining room with the mahogany walls." So I was thrilled with that, and the rest of the trip, I slept in his bunk, and nobody from my squadron could find me at night. I learned that they were looking for me the whole trip, and we had been on the ship for fifty-seven days before we arrived at our destination.

The *Conte di Savoia* was one of the largest ships in the world, with an impressive gross tonnage of over 48,000 and a length of 814 feet. The speed was not anything to be ashamed of either as the ship could claim to have surface speed of more than 27 knots.

As a troop transport in 1943, it carried troops from California to Bombay, India, in August of 1943 without the support of a convoy. After having served as a troop ship, in September 1943, just one month after we landed in Bombay, she was bombed without any means of defense and sank in shallow water.

CHAPTER XVI

Storm

WE WERE THEN back on route in the Indian Ocean. One night, we had a terrible storm, and the prow of the ship was going way up into the sky and falling down with a crash. Then it was sliding down into the water on its side and then back up into the air again and bounced down again. It was very scary. We were holding on to our cots for dear life, but nothing happened.

CHAPTER XVII

Starvation

WE GOT TWO meals a day, and on Saturday it was baked beans for breakfast. I must tell you that I threw up every day of the fifty-seven-day trip. I was sick all the way through it because when I was starving to death, after about the first week, I had to eat whether I threw up or not. One day, I crashed the line, but I didn't have the required ticket so that you could go to the line more than once. I crossed the line a lot, and throughout most of the day, I was pretty sick and then decided I would steal some food from the navy because they really ate well. So I put a T-shirt over my naked torso and walked into the kitchen so it would look like I worked there. I picked up two chops off the grill, and it burned my fingers. As I was walking out of the kitchen, the navy chief grabbed me by the neck and shoved me into the wall and took my two chops and threw them into the trash. He then threw me out of the kitchen.

Another memory I have is walking around aimlessly and finding a corridor that was fenced in by a wire fence, and you could see piles of chickens. It wasn't refrigerated, and there were bodies of dead chickens, and among them were rats and mice running around. Once I saw that, it was very hard to eat chicken again.

CHAPTER XVIII

Burlesque

THE FIRST STOP we made on our itinerary was the great Suez Canal. The first thing I noticed about the Suez Canal when we stopped at the entrance to it was a big billboard showing that there were burlesque theaters. There was a lottery for those who could get off the ship and go to the burlesque show. I didn't win but thought it was kind of odd that they would have a picture of a girl in a burlesque show on the billboard. Then we went through the Suez Canal, and it took forever as it was a very slow process going through the locks.

CHAPTER XIX

Australia Entertainment

THE NEXT STOP on our itinerary was Australia, where we docked for a couple of days. While we were on the ship, there was a group of people that seemed like a family who were singing and dancing with costumes. We were then allowed to leave the ship and go into the ocean from the nearby beach. The hilarious thing about it was you weren't allowed to wear bathing trunks, and the officers would walk around naked, wearing their hats with the bars or epauletsto show their rank. The rest of us just walked naked on the beach, which had huge rocks, so we could hardly walk. Rumor was that women who had telescopes were watching us, and I'm sure that was a better show than the burlesque show we had seen.

CHAPTER XX

New Zealand Apples

WE THEN TRAVELED to New Zealand, where we did get permission to walk around. As the ship approached the port, it was a sight to see the houses that were up on a hill with clean, shiny windows. We walked around, and it was like a suburban town. I went by a grocery store with a basket of apples outside, and I picked up one and walked into the store. I told the shopkeeper that I wanted to buy it, and he asked for $1 when it was worth only five to ten cents. I got very angry that he would ask a soldier to pay such a high price for an apple.

CHAPTER XXI

Bombay

THE NEXT MORNING, the sun came up, and it was a calm ocean once again. We then arrived in Bombay, India. We never were told where we were going. We were able to get off the ship and walk around Bombay for a short time. I went into a bar with a friend, and it was the first time I had been in a bar. I sat on a stool and ordered a rum and Coke drink, acting like I was twenty-five years old instead of eighteen years old, which I was at the time.

CHAPTER XXII

Reincarnation

AFTER GOING BACK to the ship, we gathered our belongings and disembarked down the gangplank, and we were put on trains with narrow rails. We, of course, had no idea where we were going. Every fifty miles or so, we stopped for water and would get off the train and walk around. On the train, we would see lots of roaches, and we would run around stomping on them. We were then told that we were not allowed to kill the roaches because the Indian people thought that they were their uncles who were reincarnated, and they were actually serious about it.

CHAPTER XXIII

Missionaries

ON OUR FIRST stop, there were people at the train station who were missionaries who served us coffee and donuts. I was so impressed that the missionaries were there, and they were from somewhere in Britain, but they were very nice and courteous. We were a bunch of loudmouth GIs, which was embarrassing to me.

We got back on the train and made a stop for a couple of days, where we then changed trains; this time we were unable to have a train that would fit all of us. So we were all huddled together side by side on the seats, which was very uncomfortable. At one point, I climbed up onto the baggage rack with my legs hanging over.

CHAPTER XXIV

Unload

THE TRAIN ARRIVED at the junction of the Brahmaputra River and the train station, where the natives buried their dead on flaming biers floated down the river—a horrible sight. We learned the colonel had refused native labor help in unloading the boat, instead having his troops do backbreaking work—a terrible memory to this day.

CHAPTER XXV

Jorhat, India

WE FINALLY ARRIVED in Jorhat, India, where we were to set up camp; however, there were no tents or cots. So some genius decided that seventy-six of us should sit in a complete circle back-to-back throughout the night, with no moon. We were all scared to death, waiting for the first part of World War II to affect us. The rumor was that Japanese paratroopers were in the area, but actually the only enemies we had to contend with at night were the mosquitoes, bugs, snakes, and all the other critters and vermin.

We did manage to get enough cots, tents, and supplies to make it look like a camp. The cots were rope beds with a comforter to lie on on top of the rope. This was to be our home away from home for about twelve months while we suffered through the heat and listened to the bombing, trying to sleep, which was torture.

CHAPTER XXVI

Driver's License

I LEARNED TO drive a jeep by an incompetent person who didn't tell me that you let out the clutch and give it the gas with the same pressure, so I stalled hundreds of times before I got the swing of it. Then I was able to drive around, and then, like an idiot, I graduated to a two-and-a-half-ton truck. So for the three years I was there, I would beg the army truck drivers to let me drive whenever I could. Sometimes they would let me, and I would flood the carburetor and the truck would stall intermittently. Once I was driving about fifty miles an hour going around a bend and came across an iron-trestle bridge. I hit the sides of the bridge and bounced back and forth while the truck driver turned white and insisted that I get out from behind the wheel.

Another time, I was trying to change seats with the driver while we were driving, and we just went into the bottom of the ditch. There was an incident with me driving a two-and-a-half-ton truck with about thirty GIs where we went through mud and slid into a ditch. Then I took a driver's test in a half-track, which was twenty feet high, and they gave me that because they didn't think I could pass. I was not one of the boys, so they tried to sabotage my driver's test. However, I did pass, and I could drive any type of vehicle.

CHAPTER XXVII

Chinese Friends

ONE BEAUTIFUL MORNING, I was riding in a truck with a black driver (all the truck drivers were black). Don't ask me where we were going or where we had been; we probably did this every boring day. We soon came upon a large group of Chinese infantrymen who were all over the place. As soon as they saw us, they tried to climb on the truck even though we were pretty much speeding along. Some of them even tried to throw themselves in front of the truck so we would stop; in fact, the driver gave it the gas and swerved to avoid them. Fortunately, no one was hurt. I then decided I was going to get out of the truck, and I told the driver to slow down so I could jump out of the cab. As I jumped out, my ring finger was caught on a hook that held canvas covers. The hook pierced my ring finger as I fell into a ditch. My finger bled profusely as I lay there. The Chinese were not far behind. I immediately unhooked my leather belt and loosened my medical package, which contained sulfur powder, which I knew would immediately stop the bleeding. At the same time, I heard what sounded like a hand grenade going off. Apparently, the Chinese tried to stop the truck, and I hoped they missed. When I calmed down, I staggered onto the road to make my way back to camp. The bleeding had stopped, and I didn't need to tend to it anymore except that I was somewhat woozy and a little faint.

Much later, after the war was over and I was home and discharged, my father said to me one day, "What is wrong with your finger?" Here, even though it had been two years since the accident, the tendon had apparently been severed, and the finger was growing slightly bent inward. I had never noticed it until I tried to bowl one night. My father tortured me to file a claim with the Air Corps for a disability pension. I did not because of my disillusionment with my war service. Finally he forced me to go with him to the VFW offices, where they were helping GIs with claims. Reluctantly, I filed a claim and was advised that there were no records of my injury, and I needed to have two people sign attesting to this incident. Remember, I had no medical attention officially because we had no medics. So that ended that, and no Purple Heart for me. Now, seventy years later, my finger has grown inward to its maximum, into the palm of my hand. This has been my World War II injury that has inspired stories to my children and grandchildren that have been much more elaborate than the truth.

Chinese army, infantry training

Chiang Kai-shek's Chinese army, a US ally, was instrumental in protecting B-29s returning to China from bombings in Japan.

CHAPTER XXVIII

Ennui

EVERY MORNING, WE would pack up our gear, which included a rifle, a gas mask, and a backpack with junk in it. We would often go on some meaningless mission to do nothing, looking for I don't know what, and playing war. One day, I decided we should build some buildings with wood, and we taught ourselves to make levels using string. We then used strings on sticks for the uprights and horizontal bars until we built what looked like a barn area with a matted roof. We then climbed up on top where the roof was going to be, without fear in 120-degree heat. It got so hot that somebody decided in the afternoon we shouldn't do anything until we cooled off, which we decided was a good time for a siesta every day until the cooler weather came along.

CHAPTER XXIX

Another Tragedy

WE WERE IN our tents one night, and we were called to help because a plane had crashed nearby. By the time we got to the field, the plane was on fire, and everyone was running around in an attempt to save some lives. Our medical officer received a Bronze Star Medal for running into the fire, although he was unable to save anybody. All five of the GIs were killed. The next day, we buried them, but unfortunately, about three months later, we found one of them hanging in a tree. We had buried four men in five graves. I seemed to have slipped into the war accidentally.

CHAPTER XXX

Monsoon

THEN CAME THIS horrible season where there was nothing but rain, which you know as monsoon season. Shoes floated down by the tent area and were caked with green moss. Your clothing smelled of mildew so strong that it made you choke.

One day, I decided to sell some of my cigarettes to some Chinese soldier. It was pouring rain, so they came into the tent with their ponchos on, which were ideal for them to pick up anything in the tent that wasn't nailed down. They left after paying $10 a carton for cigarettes that I had paid $1 for, but then after they left, we found that they stole everything they could get their hands on.

CHAPTER XXXI

Banded Krait Snake

SINCE WE WERE living in tents, there was little protection against all kinds of creatures. One day, a beautiful red and black snake found its way into our tent, and a Filipino national, who was a member of our squadron and apparently knew snakes better than the rest of us, picked up the snake by its throat and, with its mouth wide open, poured mosquito lotion into it and released it. The snake crazily slithered about while we jumped all over it until the Filipino stomped it dead. The next day, someone went to headquarters and found a poster showing this snake to be a banded krait, whose venom would cause death in thirty seconds—and we are still alive.

BENGAL TIGER

I was awakened one night in my tent by a rustling noise, and there facing me were two green eyes and what appeared to be some kind of animal. As I was able to focus in the darkness, it clearly became a Bengal tiger that was around five feet. I froze. It walked around my cot, sniffed, and ran out of the tent, never to be seen again. Some shots rang out from some poor marksmen. Thank goodness, it never came back.

Bengal tiger,
Myitkyina, Burma

This vicious beast—though its population is decreasing—was still lurking around in Burma, scaring the hell out of GIs, especially eighteen-year-old city boys.

CHAPTER XXXII

Cowboys and Indians

ONE DAY, ABOUT twenty of us rode in the back of a two-and-a-half-ton truck through the town and decided to shoot up the town. We rode through the marketplace and shot off our carbines in the air, screaming and yelling like cowboys and American Indians. All of a sudden, I found myself looking down the barrel of a gun into the eyes of a child about ten years old. That cured me from this behavior forever, and fortunately, nobody got hurt.

CHAPTER XXXIII

Childhood Tragedy

WE DID DUMB things like shoot at the palm trees that were put down the river to hide the enemy who were trying to escape. One day, somebody shot and it ricocheted and it hit a child standing on the banks of the river, and the child was killed. The army gave quite a bit of rupees to the family. As it turned out, every couple of days, the elders marched out onto the beach and released the children, hoping that somebody would get shot so they could get money from the army. After that, we never shot at the floating palm trees again. This is something good about the Americans; I think we would have shot at the elders, but not at the children. The Japanese were known to have children march in front of them to not be shot by the Americans.

CHAPTER XXXIV

Dumbo and Company

ANOTHER DAY, I was called by the lieutenant in charge with a job for me. I always seemed to get the dumb jobs. He said he wanted me to go with the trucks to Titabar with some Indians. He said he couldn't promise me anything from the name (ha-ha), but we were going to have some elephants load logs into the trucks for construction. So I emptied my gas mask and filled it with some fruit to take along with me for the day. Off we went with about five elephants and some Indian "off the wall" boss who taught me how to ride on the back of an elephant and make him or her respond with commands by wrapping a band to the lobe of the elephant's ear. If you push right, the elephant would turn right, and push the left ear and they would turn left. So we did that all day, and the elephants were very good. They would lift the logs with their trunks and throw them back over their heads into the trucks. One of the elephants that I was riding decided that he wasn't going to be cooperative. So he started to throw the logs every which way and reared up on his hind legs. I slid off down his back, and I hid behind the truck while the elephant went crazy. Everyone was screaming and running around like they were insane.

Asian elephants,
Titabar, India

These elephants were known by the shape of their ears, as opposed to African elephants. They were used by Indian labor forces primarily for transporting logs.

CHAPTER XXXV

Meeting a Friend/Foe

WE THEN TOOK a break and walked a path that was uphill about two feet wide around the side of a hill. I was dressed with a field backpack, rifle, and gas mask because you always had to be prepared since you never knew what could happen. As I walked up this path about one hundred feet up, I came around the bend on the hill and saw a warrior with a spear on his back, with a rifle on his shoulder, and war paint on his face, coming toward me. We saw each other at the same time, and both of us stopped in our tracks. Apparently we were both scared to death, and we both turned around and ran. If he did capture me, he would see the American flag on my back, which he would know in his hieroglyphic language that he should take me to the nearest American army camp and he would receive a lot of money for saving my life.

Gurkhas

The Gurkhas are an ethnic community from Nepal. Their name derives from the Hindu warrior-saint Guru Gorakhnath (eighth century). Gurkhas are indigenous people to India. A Gurkha is disciplined for beheading a Taliban, also known to have decapitated their enemies. During World War II, they were more or less friendly to our troops and would often bring the wounded back to our front lines and would be paid handsomely by us.

CHAPTER XXXVI

Thirty Days' Punishment

SO AFTER THIS ordeal, we went back to camp, and I found that somebody saw my gas mask without the canister, which I had removed to make room for fruit, and reported it. I was given thirty days' punishment and was not allowed to leave the camp. If I did leave, there would be some kind of solitary confinement or worse as punishment, which, in my opinion, didn't fit the crime. There were other incidents like this too numerous to mention and too stupid to comprehend, but this was what it was like in India during World War II.

CHAPTER XXXVII

Burma Next to Last

WE WERE THEN ordered to go to Burma to help the British to regain Northern Burma from the Japanese. They had lost it twice, and we got the dirty work. We flew into Burma, which was scarier because the enemy was all over the place and there was bombing nightly. By then, the US Army Air Corps had these night flares that you wouldn't see coming, and they were pretty effective. But the ground troops were more effective even though they were not combat ready. We were on a river that purified itself with a terrific current.

So then one day, I was driving a jeep on the Burma Road, and I came upon an Indian who had some eggs. He sold them for a couple of dollars each, and I was able to put some into a canteen cup, boiled them over a fire, and enjoyed boiled eggs.

Bridge over Irrawaddy River,
Myitkyina, Burma

The Irrawaddy River current was so strong that the water purified itself every foot. The Fifty-Second Air Service Squadron made it their home for thirteen months, ending in November 1943.

CHAPTER XXXVIII

Salty Kool-Aid

I WROTE HOME often to ask my mom to send me a loaf of italian bread. She didn't do that, but she did send me some Kool-Aid. A friend of mine was in charge of the officers' club, which was a makeshift, ramshackle building where the officers drank themselves silly. He said he would make the Kool-Aid while we were amusing ourselves with a group of British soldiers. I couldn't wait to drink this Kool-Aid, and he served it to us in cups. I was the first to taste it and spit it out because he used salt instead of sugar, and it was not drinkable. I wanted to kill him.

The food was not what we were used to eating when we were home, but they did give us some square cheese and bread, which was our Sunday dinner. It got so bad after a while that we had no fresh water and no food except for applesauce and pineapples. Once I stole some pineapples and took them into my tent and everybody got a piece. I got caught, of course, and again wasn't allowed outside of camp for thirty days. This wasn't really a punishment because there was no place to go except into the jungle, where you wouldn't want to go anyway.

CHAPTER XXXIX

Calcutta

SOMEHOW WE DID get a twenty-one-day leave, and we went by air to Calcutta with thoughts of American girls flying in our heads. We landed in Calcutta on January 1, 1944, and found that the commanding general had forbidden houses of prostitution as off-limits. Whereas before, the American MPs had kept watch over the GIs as they lined up outside these places. When we got there, they were off-limits, and you didn't go near those places. They did us a favor in hindsight.

We then walked aimlessly around Calcutta, and it looked like New Orleans with fancy woodwork. In the second floor of one of the buildings were two white girls leaning over the railings, telling us to come up, which was like a Christmas present. We went up to their apartment. The first thing I noticed was that there were votive candles on the shelves of every bedroom, and in the living room were religious pictures. It turned out that these girls lived with the mother of one of the girls who was a madam working out of the big hotel in Calcutta. She had a string of girls that she offered to the men that were dining in the makeshift dining room. She sold them for the night for twenty-one rupees, which was seven dollars. When I got to know her, I asked why it was twenty-one, and she said that one dollar was for tax due. She was a short, obese black woman, and her daughters were from a white British officer.

CHAPTER XL

Kitty

WE SPENT THE afternoon dancing with the girls to a phonograph and making ourselves comfortable. We made plans to meet them later that night, and we took them to dinner. My girl worked out so well that I saw her every night of the remaining fifteen days of furlough. Her name was Kathryn Bentley, and I don't think it would be off-limits to reveal her name at this point, but she was called Kitty. She liked my dancing, and we got along very well. One night, we went to the movies, and it was set up to have the more expensive box seats in the back of the theater. They had sofa seats in front of the box seats that looked like they were there if you wanted to fool around. The cheaper seats, which were one or two cents, were just to sit on the floor in the front. Of course, I paid for the box seats, which were the most expensive.

As I said, she really liked me and wanted me to impress her mother. So that night she told me to come over on her birthday. She gave me a piece of expensive jewelry and told me to go to a store and have it wrapped so that I could bring it when I came over for her birthday. She said that her mother would be more receptive to me. She didn't like her daughter to associate with American GIs, for which I didn't blame her. Kitty was only about eighteen years old, which was about my age at the time. I went to the jewelry store, and sure enough, they wrapped up the jewelry for me in a fancy box. I brought the present with me, and her mother was overjoyed that I gave it to her.

Once that happened, her mother liked me, and I spent my time in and out of her apartment. Her mother had a boyfriend named Morris while her husband was away fighting in the war. He was an old British reporter and retired soldier who was a very friendly guy, and I worked my way into both of their good graces. I spent my days horseback riding on a horse that Morris had, and her mother even got me a new saddle. While other GIs were walking around Calcutta aimlessly, I was having great times with Kitty and riding horses. Later I told everyone that Kitty was Merle Oberon, who had been born in China and then migrated to India and Burma before she went to Hollywood to become an actress. Nobody believes me.

One night, I borrowed a hotel key from a friend of mine who allowed me to use it to take Kitty to the hotel, which I did. We went into the room, and she disrobed and got in bed. While I was doing the same thing, there was a knock on the door, and it was my friend who had the hotel room and a British soldier. Both were drunk and demanded to be let in the room. I wouldn't let them in, but they kept pounding on the door, so I finally let them in. They came in and sat on the other bed staring at Kitty. I tried to convince them to leave, but they wouldn't. She begged them to turn the light out so she could get out of bed and into the bathroom for her clothes. They finally agreed and the lights were turned off, and she ran into the bathroom and got dressed. We both left, and I never forgave my friend who ruined my best night.

So in all these three weeks, I never culminated my romance with Kitty, even though I tried my best.

CHAPTER XLI

No Chutes

IT WAS TIME for my furlough to end and to head back to Burma, so we went to the airfield to find that there were airplanes that had crashed all over the airfield. So then we got on an airplane at night, which was eerie since we couldn't see much, and it was the middle of the war. The cargo was strapped to the floor, and then the copilot came back to us and said, "I hate to tell you, but there are no parachutes, and we are flying into a bad storm. We are flying into mountains, and we can't see much of anything." Looking back on this, it seems to me that I should've been scared out of my wits.

CHAPTER XLII

Kitty Again

SIX MONTHS LATER, I returned to Calcutta and reunited with Kitty, my true love. A friend of mine, who was with me at the time, giggled hysterically that I was like an old sea captain coming back to port for his woman. The second trip, I left after one night, having finally consummated our love. I had reservations in a fancy hotel in Darjeeling for three weeks. It was a British vacation destination at the foot of Mount Everest. I tried to convince Kitty to come with me, but her mother wouldn't allow it. So I left her, and as I was leaving, two MPs came into her apartment and arrested me because they had recently listed that street on the out-of-bounds area. So they took my friend and me to an MP prison. As we were taken into the jail, a bell rang and it was time to eat, and so we didn't go into the cell. We noticed an open door, and we ducked into the open door, which was a cadre mess hall. We sat down and ate. At the end of the meal, we didn't know where to go, and as we walked around, a sergeant said, "Where have you been, we have been looking all over for you." My friend had the presence of mind to ask for his right "to see the officer of the day," like a phone call back home. The officer of the day was called, and my friend, who was 6'5" and weighed about two hundred fifty pounds, started to cry with tears coming down his face. "This is my first furlough after two and a half years in the jungle, please don't send us back." The OD called an MP and said, "Take these two to the railroad station and wait for the train to leave, and don't come back to Calcutta." So if it weren't for my friend, we would have been back to the jungle.

CHAPTER XLIII

Darjeeling

WHEN WE ARRIVED in Darjeeling, we were late, and my date ran off with the trumpet player from the US Air Force Band. She was about twenty years older than I was, and the next day, she was arrested by the Indian police for trying to poison her husband. That was the end of her.

During my stay, there were lots of dances with high school students and their mother chaperones. I met a cute fifteen-year-old whose mother invited me to join them for Mass the next day, which was Sunday. I walked over to the Catholic church, and after Mass we had breakfast served by the nuns. We then went to their house and visited. They then invited me to stay for dinner, which was served by their servants, and I met the father, who was an Indian officer, who was not too pleased at my being there. It was a thrill to be sitting in real chairs and sofas after being in the jungle for such a long time.

I went back to the fancy hotel and shortly teamed up with some nurses who were older than us. One of them even had a gray streak of hair down the middle of her head. The two nurses invited me and my friend to their hotel room, where we spent most of the night drinking a bottle of scotch worth $80 a bottle, facing each other on twin beds. The most I did was put my arm around my nurse, and my friend sat down and did nothing. It was the last night of their furlough; I don't know what we were thinking. The next day, we rode horseback to the train station to see them off.

Nothing much happened the rest of the furlough, and we flew back to our base located in Myitkyina.

CHAPTER XLIV

Bathtub

ONE OF THE most memorable purchases I made was when a commanding general said that he wanted a real bathtub. So I spent a couple of days looking for a real bathtub. Can you imagine? Maybe he should have sent us to look for some food instead. I finally found one and brought it back for him, and it cost a lot of money, which was even more ridiculous since there was no plumbing. Then he had some yard birds fill it with buckets of water. He then sent me on many trips to buy things that we didn't need and didn't really use. I got to know the merchants quite well in every store. I would sit in a chair in the middle of the store in front of an electric fan to cool off in the hundred-degree heat. Because I got friendly with these merchants and I wanted to learn their language, they helped me by giving me books on the Hindustani and American translation. One thing they were very serious about was to find out how I could send their sons to the United States to become doctors. I heard that from every merchant I ever met, and sixty years later, there are thousands and thousands of male and female Indian doctors in the United States.

CHAPTER XLV

Horseback Rides

WE HAD A psychiatric medical unit in the area, and one of the things that they did was to help these poor GIs who were losing their minds either from the torture of their living conditions or the monotony and boredom. They had lots of playthings for these patients, and the biggest plaything that they had was not one but several horses. These poor guys didn't want to ride around and enjoy themselves, which was lucky for me, because I was able to bargain with them and occasionally got to ride the horses. One Sunday, I rode a horse to Mass and left the horse outside in the sun. The other GIs let me know how stupid I was to leave the horse outside with the sun bearing down.

CHAPTER XLVI

Donkeys

ONE DAY, WE noticed activity in the hills. About one hundred mountain troops were coming down the hills riding on their steady, sure jackasses. They had been holed up in the hills for about two years, and we didn't even know they were there. With the end of the war near, they were coming out of their campsites. Seeing their long beards, they looked like real western cowboys. I made myself known to them and was able to bargain with them, and they let me ride their donkeys in exchange for getting some film printed for them, which they were unable to do. They had a lot of rolls of film that needed to get printed.

There were a lot of GIs walking down the road of Mandalay hundreds of miles. I met one of these kids when I was in New Zealand. He was eighteen and I was twenty by then, and he thought that Myitkyina (michinaw) was a good place to be. Then I was told I was going to be promoted from corporal to staff sergeant, which was a good promotion according to the leadership. I was soon to be promoted to first sergeant.

CHAPTER XLVII

Hobby

THERE WAS A young kid about ten years old who grew up hanging around us and was a great table tennis player, which is what we would do while we were waiting for our orders. One of the squadron commanders, who was around fifty, said he was going to adopt the boy. He had enough points to go back to the United States and left the boy with his friend until he could come back and officially adopt him. He had arranged for the adoption when he returned in thirty days. Unfortunately, his plane crashed, and we got word that the boy was now left alone without a father or stepfather. It saddened us more than anything else we had seen in real wartime, like plane crashes with our friend aboard and other types of tragedies.

I became very good at Ping-Pong and played in several competitions and was so good that I came in second. I was supposed to be sent to another competition in Calcutta, but it was called off when the war ended.

CHAPTER XLVIII

Burma Hijacking

NEAR THE END of the war, I was given another random assignment. There were lots of convoys on the Burma Road, where the trucks would arrive at their destinations empty or half-empty. The truck drivers were selling the cargo, or it was being stolen while they slept; of course, they knew nothing. So it was my job to fly with them to the top of the Burma Road in Lido, where they would be given a loaded truck and a manifest. I would stay in Lido, where I waited for the next truck drivers to fly there. While I was there, I slept in a tent with a drunk major, who was drunk almost every night and insisted I drink with him. He didn't care what my rank was; he just wanted company. I hated every minute of it. It finally came to an end when a "sting operation" caught the truck drivers selling the cargo to Indians on the Burma Road.

CHAPTER XLIX

VE Day

SHORTLY AFTER THAT assignment, an announcement was made that the war in Europe was over. I think that was in July of 1945, and several months later, an announcement was made that the atom bomb was dropped on Hiroshima; and a few days later, another atom bomb was dropped on another Japanese city, killing thousands of people. The war in Japan was now over.

It would appear that this was a happy time; it really wasn't. Everyone was so fed up that it was just another incident, and there was no clapping of hands. This was especially so since at the end of the European war, we were told that we would be here a long time and that there was more killing to be done and to be killed. As it turned out, a few weeks later, we were on our way home. That was the irony and tragedy of the war experience. Can you imagine that there were some soldiers in Europe that were sent to India to continue their army service even though the war was practically over? They had been in campaigns in Europe and expected to continue just like nothing happened. It was really disheartening.

CHAPTER L

Poor Nurses

PLANES WERE LEAVING every two minutes filled with nurses, and the GIs wanted to get on those planes with the nurses. We were not allowed on the planes with the nurses, much to our dismay. So we boarded another plane which took off directly behind the plane of nurses. When the plane in front of us got to Taj Mahal, the pilot banked the wings to the left so the nurses could see the beautiful sight. Unfortunately, the pilot lost control and crashed to the ground, and the nurses were all killed. It was a stroke of fate that is difficult to contemplate.

Taj Mahal,
Agra, India

One of the Seven Wonders of the World built by a famous rajah for one of his wives. Visited by thousands of tourists every year.

Army Nurse Corps
uniform, 1944–1945

This picture shows a group of nurses belonging to the 250th station hospital. Note the nurses are wearing cotton seersucker uniforms with appropriate caps and are draped in what appears to be the old dark-blue capes.

CHAPTER LI

Karachi Seaport

WHEN WE ARRIVED at our destination, Karachi, a seaport, we were eventually to board a troop ship, the *Cat Ballou*, where we were shaken down for any valuables that could not be taken with us to the United States. Such things as watches, radios, fleece-lined bombardier jackets—things that the officers thought should not be left to the Indians—were burned in piles. I tried to smuggle a fleece-lined jacket and was caught and had to give it up.

While we were waiting to board the ship, which took about three months, I was quartered in a private room with a shower in the best part of the barracks, due to my rank. This was quite a high point in the life I had led in Myitkyina (michinaw). During this interminable wait, there was nothing to be done but play table tennis and sit around. One day, I saw a check-off list for church dividing us into the three major religions—Catholics to go to Mass on Sunday in the desert, Jewish to go to synagogue in Karachi, which was a metropolitan city, and Protestants to go to service in the desert. Of course, I checked off Hebrew, and best of all, every night, I was given a jeep and drove to town and met Jewish GIs and civilians, both men and women. I got back into civilization, which included social activities and dances. It was like heaven, especially during Hanukah because there were parties, dances, and gifts, which I hadn't experienced for three years. During this period, I didn't even think of home.

CHAPTER LII

Going Home

IT WAS FINALLY time to board the ship home to the United States. I was numb with relief; it was like being in a coma. I wasn't thinking of my parents or my brother or anything. It wasn't a homecoming that I could be happy about or could even think about. It was like the end of some death. The emotion was covered by the fact, and since we never knew exactly when we were going home, when it was finally here, it took away the joy.

We left port December 21, 1945, and arrived in New York City January 1, 1946. As soon as we walked up the gangplank, we were told to get in the chow line. We could eat whatever and as much as we wanted. There was milk and bread and other types of American food that we hadn't had for three years. Most of us ate like pigs, and I myself had two meals in a row.

After the first meals, we were herded down into the bowels of the ship. There was a chief petty officer who was overweight, and it was evident that he had been well fed despite the war. He announced that he had chosen our troop to be given KP duty on the entire trip home because we were the backbone of the Army Air Corps. A short time later, an announcement was made asking for volunteers to work on the ship's newspaper. You needed to be able to type and work on stencils, etc. I was up on the bridge in a flash and volunteered, spending the next ten days being a "reporter" on the ship. I didn't even bother to sleep in my bunk because I was afraid I would get pulled out for KP. So I slept on two chairs put together and had a very sore back after all that time. I interviewed the lieutenant commander of the navy, who was not very pleased to be interviewed by a staff sergeant. I asked him about the ship and if it had been in any battles, but he wasn't very pleasant and full of himself. He wouldn't even answer most of my questions, so I made up stuff. I just did this to get out of KP, so I didn't really care.

CHAPTER LIII

Stringer

I TRIED TO keep myself busy to make the paper look good. So I wrote some fiction about two Chinese GIs named Ping and Pong who invented table tennis, and they did it in the water, which made it water polo. It was very funny, and I was proud of it. It went over pretty well on the ship, and people congratulated me about the story.

One day, a ship came alongside of us and slowed down. The code man was flashing signals at us, and I was very impressed with the people around me that could understand the code signals. They told me that they were saying "Have a happy Christmas and New Year," and I wished I had learned it.

CHAPTER LIV

Movie Time—Nice Marines

DURING THE CROSSING, we were not allowed to watch the movies that the Navy captain and his crew enjoyed. So of course, you would expect that I would sneak in and get caught. I was thrown out by a vulgar marine.

Christmas came and went without much fanfare. We knew we were on our way home, but people didn't care much about the holiday. The days just overlapped. Then we got to New Year's Eve, and you would have thought that there would have been something bawdy and ribald, but nothing of the sort happened. A sailor approached me about midnight and offered me two slices of bread with American cheese for $5. I was angry that he would make me have to buy a sandwich, but I was hungry, so I gave him the $5 and then dropped it on the deck instead of handing it to him.

CHAPTER LV

Happy New Year

HAPPY NEW YEAR! We sighted the Statue of Liberty and passed a life buoy manned by a Jewish man who sat in this thing all night. It was named something like Abraham Buoy. They had somebody do this for every ship that came back from the war to New York Harbor.

We landed in New York on the Hudson River and horns were blasting, and I climbed up to get a good view. Unfortunately, my right eardrum was damaged, resulting in scar tissue that decreased my hearing ability.

We were herded back to our bunks and waited until our names were called. Then, we climbed up with our duffel bags, and we disembarked. We were led to a ferry boat on the water, which had been used for automobiles so that the decks were concave so you couldn't stand on it. When the boat sped away, we all fell. We arrived in New Brunswick, which was the army base where we were going to be discharged. When the ferry came to a stop, we stumbled out onto the gangplank, some with broken and sprained ankles. Fortunately, I was not one of them. We were paraded like animals onto a field and made to march like soldiers into an army barracks. We were told in no uncertain terms not to attempt to escape and that it would delay everyone. If anyone did that, we would have to start over and could be delayed for months. We went to our cots, and a good friend of mine and I climbed over the barbed wire fence.

A married couple drove by as we were walking and skidded to a stop and asked us if we wanted a ride. We said yes and asked them to take us to the nearest highway. The driver sped away, obviously with intent to help us, when we saw in the rearview mirror an Army Air Corps MP station wagon coming up behind us with its lights blinking. This civilian driver and his family were experienced with this and outdistanced the MPs and went up some side roads. We lost the MP, and the driver took us to a highway and let us out and said, "That will be $5," and I said, "—— $5," and he got nothing. My friend thought he should get $2, but here we were back in the United States after three years being in a terrible war and someone helped us and wanted to be paid for their help. We walked to a tavern where we went in for a beer and to clean ourselves up.

So after a sandwich and a beer, we found a nearby bus stop that was going directly to Philadelphia. And of all things, it stopped at 15th and Market Streets, the location of the Penn Station. During the ride, I went to the driver and begged him to stop so I could go to the bathroom. I ran into the woods, and the entire busload got a kick out of me doing this. We arrived at the Penn Station, and I hailed a cab driver, who wouldn't take me home because he wouldn't be able to get a fare back. Here it was, my first day back in the United States, and this was how I was being treated, so I argued with him and tried to grab him by the neck. He then gave in and took me home.

CHAPTER LVI

Home!

MY FATHER AND uncle, who had no idea that I was back in the United States and in Philadelphia, were both outside, and when they saw me, my father almost fainted. He shouted to my mother, who was upstairs, and I hugged them and went in the house. My mother tried to change her clothes to put on Chinese pajamas that I had sent her. My mother cooked spaghetti and meatballs at 11 p.m., and we had a good reunion. My father, mother, uncle, and I were very happy.

I couldn't believe I hadn't seen them for three years. After having this dinner of my favorite foods, we made our way to Penn Station to make my way back to New Brunswick, New Jersey. I got on a bus and went back to the base. The MPs got on the bus and asked everyone for their papers. I sat looking straight ahead, and the MP walked by and let me go. I went to my bunk, and the next day I was on my way to discharge. I was told that I would be held back because I never got a Good Conduct Medal. They gave me a physical because I had lost eighty pounds and wanted to send me to the hospital, which I refused. So they kept me there because they didn't know what to do about the Good Conduct Medal. They finally gave up and paraded me to the lieutenant, who gave me the Good Conduct Medal. Then, I was discharged and on my way to Harrisburg to head back to Philadelphia.

The train dropped me off with my heavy duffel bag at a streetcar, which took me to my parents' home, where they were waiting for me with open arms. My brother was also there, and we had another reunion with more delicious food. I was a different person and felt like I had never been gone. The first thing I did was throw my army uniform away. I didn't want to see it anymore. I heard that other people loved their uniforms and wore it for weeks or months, whereas I wanted to be finished with this episode of my life. A few months later, one of my uncles also left the holding area prior to being discharged, and he didn't get caught either.

CHAPTER LVII

Foolhardy

DURING THE WRITING of *Lost Youth*, I purposely did not include the following incident due to my embarrassment in not wanting to reveal my stupidity in this case. However, I think it is worthwhile sharing, so here goes.

One night, my best friend, who came to my tent every night, said, "Will this ever end?" After saying this, he further said, "I have a great idea." I listened, and you won't believe his idea. He and I would break into the headquarters tent and use their equipment, including stencils, to make up the next day's orders for the day, which was to include the both of us to be flown to Calcutta and whatever stops it took to get us to New York. This would end our Air Corps careers, not thinking for a minute that we might land in Leavenworth for twenty years. We did this and the next morning left our belongings on the banks of the Irrawaddy River, hoping we might have been thought drowned. We hitched a ride to Air Transport Command to get a flight to Calcutta with these phony orders. The dispatcher was nonplussed by these orders, and we were told to have a seat and he would get to us as soon as he could. We both sat there like idiots all day, not once thinking of the foolhardiness of this scheme. By the end of the day, the dispatcher called us to tell us, without any priority in our orders, he was unable to get us a flight, but that tomorrow he was sure he could. We hitched back to the river where nobody had missed us, gathered our belongings, and with our tails between our legs headed back to our tents, maybe to see New York only if the war miraculously ended.

Looking back on this, it seems odd that the two of us never mentioned it again. After the war, I did see him, when we hysterically reminisced the whole thing.

It is doubtful if an attempt this stupid was ever duplicated by anyone.

EPILOGUE

I CAN THINK of and recall many more events and incidents that are either too raunchy or disgusting or merely uninteresting. If you want to hear gory tales, read *D-Day* or *Kelly's Heroes*.

Some of these revelations are not accurate enough to be considered factual, and my eighty-eight-year-old memory might have taken some liberties. This experience, factual or not, made me realize at a very young age that life is not wasted on the youth. I might have lost my youth, but I gained an appreciation for living.

Shoulder patch worn by all American GIs in the China Burma India Theater of war during World War II.

Made in the USA
Coppell, TX
29 January 2022

72596946R00059